Leisure

Heinemann

Schools Library and Information Service

S00000613055

First published in Great Britain by Heinemann Library
Halley Court, Jordan Hill, Oxford OX2 8EJ
a division of Reed Educational and Professional Publishing Ltd

OXFORD FLORENCE PRAGUE MADRID ATHENS
MELBOURNE AUCKLAND KUALA LUMPUR SINGAPORE TOKYO
IBADAN NAIROBI KAMPALA JOHANNESBURG GABORONE
PORTSMOUTH NH CHICAGO MEXICO CITY SAO PAULO

Designed by **AMR**
Illustrations by Art Construction
Originated in the UK by Dot Gradations Ltd, Wickford
Printed in the UK by Jarrold Printing Ltd, Thetford

02 01 00 99 98
10 9 8 7 6 5 4 3 2 1

ISBN 0 431 06453 9
This is also available in a hardback library edition (ISBN 0 431 06452 0)

British Library Cataloguing in Publication Data
Rowe, Julian
    Leisure. – (Making science work)
    1. Leisure – Juvenile literature 2. Science – Juvenile
    literature
    I. Title
    790'.015

Acknowledgements
The publishers would like to thank the following for permission to reproduce photographs.

Tony Stone Images: p.4, p.5, p.9, p.10, p.14, p.15, p.24; Science Photo Library: p.8, p.12; Zefa: p.12, p.23, p.26, p.28; Topham Picturepoint: p.13; Image Bank: p.17; Frank Spooner Pictures: p.18; Sipa Press: p.19; Allsport: p.20; Hulton Deutsch: p.23; Peter Bentley/PPL: p.25; Action-Plus: p.27

Cover photograph reproduced with the permission of Berry Bingel/Ace Photo Agency.

Our thanks to Jim Drake for his comments in the preparation of this book.

Every effort has been made to contact copyright holders of any material reproduced in this book. Any omissions will be rectified in subsequent printings if notice is given to the Publisher.

CONTENTS

INTRODUCTION

Did you ever think that having fun could have anything to do with science? If not, then think again. The world of leisure is all about enjoying free time, but many of our pastimes would not be possible without the help of science. The benefits of science are everywhere. We take it for granted that we can have entertainment in our homes at the flick of a switch. Even outdoor activities such as hiking and sailing need science to help make better and safer equipment. But leisure pastimes have not always been so high-tech. So what did our ancestors do for entertainment?

In the past

Our earliest ancestors probably had very little time for leisure. They spent most of their lives searching for food and shelter. But we know that in about 3000 BC, the Ancient Egyptians began to use music and dance as part of religious rituals, to ask for the gods' protection against evil, or for success in hunting. In this way, music and dance gradually became part of daily life, and much later people began to enjoy these activities for their own sakes.

In around 3000 BC, Ancient Egyptian priests also began to act out the tales of the gods. However, it was the Ancient Greeks who actually invented the theatre. These great open-air theatres had rows of stone seats, arranged in tiers like a modern sports stadium. This seating arrangement gave everyone in the audience (up to 15,000 people) a good view. Prizes were awarded for the best plays, rather like the modern Oscar nominations.

ACOUSTICS

Greek theatres were skilfully designed and constructed to have good **acoustics**. This means that sound from the stage could be heard clearly by everyone in the audience, no matter where they sat. Even the smallest sounds could be heard right at the back!

Entertainment and sport today

The world of leisure has not changed overnight. Over the years, new developments in science and technology have been applied to traditional sports and leisure pastimes, to help enthusiasts play harder, go faster, and push themselves further than ever before. New materials such as carbon fibre, titanium and Gortex have been invented, to make lighter and stronger equipment for outdoor activities. As a result, dangerous sports such as white-water rafting and paragliding are safer than they have ever been. Science and technology have also opened up a whole new world of entertainment, including television, video cameras, computer games and techno-toys. This book looks at how the world of leisure has changed with the help of new advances in science and technology.

Surfboards are designed and sculpted with great care. It takes skill and years of practice to become this good at surfing!

Equipment you can trust is essential in climbing, however skilful a climber you might be.

ALL THE FUN OF THE FAIR

What scientific principles are at work in the fairground? Perhaps you enjoy a bumpy ride on the dodgems. You may prefer the stomach-churning roller coaster. In the Middle Ages, fairs were places where merchants sold their goods, and travelling entertainers put on sideshows. Today's fairgrounds offer visitors a host of exciting computer games and breathtaking rides, as well as traditional sideshows, swings and roundabouts. How do these games and rides work? How do we know that they are safe? Science gives us the answers.

The first Ferris Wheel was erected at Midway, Chicago, USA, in 1893. It was 76 metres across and had 36 cars, each seating 60 people. It was named after its inventor, George Ferris.

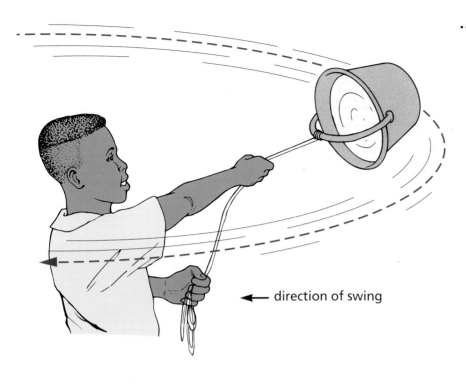

← direction of swing

You can whirl a bucket of water on a string around in a circle without spilling a drop. As you swing you will feel a pull, or force, on the end of the string. This is called **centripetal** force. If you swing the bucket fast enough, this force is stronger than the force of gravity and keeps the water in the bucket. This same force keeps you safely in your seat on roller coasters that loop-the-loop.

Gravity is the force of attraction between Earth and all objects on Earth's surface. It pulls everything in towards the centre of the planet. Without gravity everything on Earth, including you, would be weightless and float off into space!

Gravity exists between all objects in the Universe, but it is greatest for very heavy and large objects like the Sun. Its gravity pulls on all the planets in the Solar System, and keeps them moving around, or orbiting, the Sun. Gravity also keeps the Moon orbiting the Earth.

More circles

Some fairground rides allow you to experience a kind of 'artificial gravity'. You step inside a round, steel cage and stand with your back to the wall. The cage begins to rotate, then moves faster and faster. The floor gradually moves down, so that there is nothing left to stand on. But the rotating cage creates 'artificial gravity' – a force that keeps you firmly held against the wall.

ESCAPE FROM GRAVITY

In 1968, Frank Borman, James Lovell and William Anders set out to travel to the Moon and back, in the space craft *Apollo 10*. They were the first people to escape from the Earth's gravity.

THEME PARKS

If you want to say 'hello' to Mickey Mouse, visit a Viking village, meet a dinosaur or catch a thrilling ride that ends in a big splash, where would you go? A theme park, of course! Theme parks are a world apart, dedicated to providing fun and entertainment. But they are also wonderful examples of how real scientific principles, and the very latest developments in technology, can be made to work for the world of leisure.

When you enter the Magic Kingdom at Disney World, anything seems possible. Thrilling rides and exciting adventures with Disney characters are made possible through the latest scientific developments, such as virtual reality.

The geodesic golf ball, 'Spaceship Earth' at Disney World in Florida, is made of a steel framework covered with nearly 1000 triangular **aluminium** panels. It stands 55 metres high, and is supported on three pairs of concrete legs. It is built using geodesic principles, to make the structure very strong and rigid. Inside, visitors are taken on a spiral ride through a display of important events in human history.

SPACESHIP EARTH

The geodesic golf ball, 'Spaceship Earth', at Disney World in Florida, USA, takes its name from the science of geodesy, which is all about curved lines. A curved line is the shortest distance between two points on a curved surface. Geodesy is used to study and map the surface of the world. It provides information which can be used in building, engineering and navigation.

Virtual rides

A Star Tours adventure at Disneyland takes you on a fantastic journey into outer space, without ever leaving a Disney theme park. The ride makes you feel as if you are really travelling through the stars in a spaceship. It does this by tricking your body into thinking it is moving. This is easier to do than you might expect. When you look out of a train window and see the train on the next track pull out, it often feels as if you are moving – in the other direction. **Virtual** rides make use of this sensation. 'Space travellers' sit in an auditorium – the spaceship – which can be moved about in different directions. Here, they watch a specially-shot film of outer space. Each movement on the film screen is matched by the movement of the auditorium. The resulting experience is a ride that gives the illusion of actual space travel.

MOUNTAIN BIKE MANIA

There has been an explosion in the popularity of cycling in the past ten years, particularly with the arrival of new sports such as mountain biking. Mountain biking began in the US. Cyclists loaded their ordinary bicycles into the back of pick-up trucks, drove up mountain trails and rode down as fast as they could. The sport soon became very popular, so bicycle manufacturers began to use new technology to develop tough, lightweight bikes to suit the rough terrain.

Mountain bike frames

Mountain bike frames need to be light, but very strong. These days they are made from strengthened metals such as steel, **aluminium** and titanium. Some frames are even made out of highly specialized materials, such as carbon fibre, which are used to build racing cars and space shuttles. The shape of mountain bike frames makes them easy and comfortable to ride.

....

This rider is wearing a safety helmet, protective clothing and shoes. Off-road bikes have wide handlebars to give the rider more control. The space between the frame and the wheels on a mountain bike is wider than on ordinary bikes and the wheels have no mudguards, to stop mud clogging them up.

Gears for all terrain

Mountain bikes have lots of gears – 18, 21 or 24, depending on the terrain. The low gears help the rider tackle even the steepest slopes. In a low gear, the pedals turn around very easily but the rider has to turn the pedals many times to cover a short distance. In a high gear the rider needs to make fewer pedal turns to cover the same distance, but it is harder work. High gears are used downhill, where the terrain is smoother, to help the rider pick up speed and go even faster.

Put on the brakes!

Mountain bikers go extremely fast, so their brakes need to be powerful. Ordinary mountain bikes have brakes which work using steel **cables**. When you put the brakes on, the steel cables pull on the **cantilevers**. These push the brake pads against the wheel rims and slow the bike down. Downhill racing machines need very powerful hydraulic brakes, similar to those used in cars. When you put the brakes on, oil is forced down a tube and pushes the brake pads onto the wheel rim. With a hydraulic system, the brakes can be applied very hard, to stop the bicycle smoothly and efficiently.

PENNY-FARTHING

The Victorians also had a bicycle to cover rough terrain! The penny-farthing, invented in 1871 by James Starley, had a large front wheel which enabled the rider to cover rough ground at high speed. The diameter of the front wheel was about 1–1.5 metres, depending on how long the rider's legs were. Modern bicycles have smaller wheels and air-filled tyres to give a far smoother ride.

The most advanced mountain bike has a frame constructed from large-diameter aluminium tubes. The rounded, hollow shape makes them light and rigid. Front and rear suspensions smooth out the ride. The steering bearings are sealed against dirt and over-size for strength. As the rider changes the gears, they click precisely from one cog to the next.

BACKPACKING

At the end of the day, when you put up the tent and light the stove, all the hard work of backpacking can seem worth while. If you have the right kit, that is! Modern outdoor clothing, boots and equipment are made from strong, lightweight materials, using the latest technology. As a result, backpacking is a leisure activity people all round the world enjoy – no matter what the weather.

Boots made for walking

For short, easy walks, trainers or walking shoes will do. But on rough terrain hikers need strong, comfortable walking boots to support their ankles, with stiff boot soles. Stiff soles help to prevent feet and ankles rolling from side to side, and protect the soles of the feet against stony ground. Try this simple test. Bend a walking boot from heel to toe. You should be able to do this, but not too easily. Then try to twist the heel in the opposite direction from the toe: it should not move more than about one centimetre.

Burdock seeds.

VELCRO

In 1949 a Swiss engineer, Georges de Mestral, looked through his microscope at the burdock seeds that clung to his clothing. He noticed each seed had tiny hooks that caught easily on fabric. By 1957 Mestral had invented a new product called Velcro. It consists of two nylon strips. One is covered with thousands of small hooks, the other one with even smaller loops. When pressed together these strips stick to each other, but they can also be pulled apart easily and re-used.

Fabrics that breathe

When you get wet you lose heat quickly and can get very cold. This is because water draws heat away from your body about 25 times quicker than air. So it is important to stay as dry as possible when you are out in the cold, wind or rain. Plastic fabrics, made out of nylon for example, get as wet inside from trapped **perspiration** as the outside does from rain. This has led to the development of all sorts of new waterproof materials to keep us dry and warm. Today's waterproof fabrics, such as Gortex, 'breathe'. They have millions of tiny pores (holes) in them that let perspiration pass through from the inside, but not rain water from the outside.

Carrying equipment

A strong rucksack with zipped pockets and waist straps is an essential piece of equipment for any serious backpacker. After all, there is a lot to carry – a tent, sleeping bag, camping stove, compass, first-aid kit, spare clothing, maps, utensils, and food and drink. Explorers used to need a team of people to carry all the heavy gear. Now, outdoor gear is made from special lightweight material, which will fold up to fit in a very small space. Just one person can carry or pull on a sledge all they need to cross the Antarctic!

ENERGY LEVELS

Scientists measure energy in **kilojoules** (kJ). You need more than 16,000 kJ for one day's hill walking – a chocolate bar can contain 990 kJ.

This tent is made from waterproofed **synthetic** fabric, with sealed seams to stop water getting in. Flexible **aluminium** or **fibreglass** poles will support the tent in strong winds.

THE EDGE

Do you enjoy setting yourself a challenge? How far do you push yourself? There are some people who will always want to push themselves further, go faster, travel to places and do things that most of us would consider too dangerous. Top sailboarders and white-water canoeists can be like this. There is a whole range of leisure activities that people take part in quite deliberately because they are thrilling and dangerous – they want to be at the edge. In these tests of skill and courage the appliance of science is particularly important.

A big elastic band

Have you ever seen bungee jumpers dive from platforms high up in the air, plunge towards the Earth, only to bounce back up again just before their heads hit the ground? It may reassure you to learn that there is in fact a science to bungee jumping. A bungee jumper is attached to the platform by an elastic rope. When the jumper leaves the platform, his or her weight stretches the rope. It will always stretch the same amount for the same jumper. A lighter person will stretch it less than a heavier one. Bungee jumpers use three vital pieces of information – the length of the rope, the height of the jump and the weight of the jumper – to calculate exactly how long the rope needs to be for each person to make a safe jump.

White-water rafting through the Grand Canyon. Here, waves can be 5 metres high. The tough, inflatable raft must be steered past rocks and through rapids.

These skydivers are forming a ring as they fall freely through the air. When they open their parachutes it increases air resistance, and they return safely to the ground.

BUNGEE JUMP

Bungee jumpers use Hooke's law to make their jumping calculations. This law states that a heavy object stretches a spring twice as much as an object weighing half as much, and so on. The law was discovered by an English scientist and architect called Robert Hooke (1635–1703), who did a lot of research into weights and springs.

FREE FALL

You might think that any falling object would pick up speed as it falls, until it hits the ground. Falling objects do pick up speed as they fall, but only until they reach a speed of about 193 kph (130 mph). Then **friction**, or air pushing against the falling object, stops it going any faster. This speed is called the terminal velocity. Skydivers stop falling any faster when they reach terminal velocity. They open their parachutes to return safely to the ground.

COMPUTER CRAZY

Did you know that one Ancient Egyptian Pharaoh had a version of noughts and crosses chiselled into the wall of his tomb, so that he could play in the afterlife? People have been playing board games for at least 4000 years. Today, all these games can be played on computer, or on a television screen, by simply plugging in controls called **games consoles**. The very first successful video game was *Space Invaders*, which dates from 1978. The makers used a familiar idea from the world of games, whereby the player has to destroy enemy invaders, but this time the computer was the opponent. This, together with the **graphics** and sound effects, gave an old idea a whole new lease of life.

Human brain versus computer

Some computer games are like traditional board games, such as draughts or chess. At first, computer chess programs were easily beaten by human chess champions. Now the best chess programs sometimes beat the champion. The computer cannot 'think' like a chess player, but the computer chess program is designed to work out the results of all the possible moves it, and the human player, can make.

COMPUTER GAMES

Computer programs give instructions to a computer or games console. The instructions are carried as long chains of numbers. These chains are coded in **binary digits** or 'bits' – a method of counting that uses only ones and noughts. The longer the chain, the more instructions it carries. The most powerful computers and consoles are able to handle longer number chains faster. The latest games consoles can handle 32-bit numbers very quickly.

Board games need only simple **graphics**, but some games demand a powerful and fast computer to make the images you see appear real.

Armchair hi-tech

Some games, such as those that **simulate** flying an aeroplane, have very detailed graphics, and need powerful equipment to make the images appear real. Video consoles plugged into an ordinary television screen can give this kind of quality. The newest machines have CD-quality sound, can generate 16 million different colours and operate at amazingly high speed. How do they do this?

The latest desk-top computers have millions of parts called **transistors** that decode, or process, many hundreds of instructions from a computer program. Consoles have a special RISC (Reduced Instruction Set Computing) chip. This chip needs more instructions than those in an ordinary desk-top computer, but they are simpler. This means that the computer can carry out the instructions far more quickly.

What's next?

Some arcade games use **virtual reality** to make the players feel as if they are part of the images they see. The players wear headsets that show slightly different images to each eye. This creates the illusion of a three-dimensional scene, that the player can move about in.

Playing an arcade game that uses virtual reality to make the player feel that they are in a three-dimensional scene.

BIG POOLS, LITTLE POOLS

Some swimmers take pride in breaking the ice in order to enjoy their midwinter swim – but you're probably not one of them! Most people prefer to swim in warmer waters in the sunshine, or in an indoor pool where the weather doesn't matter. Elaborate water parks with artificial warm climates are becoming very popular in places where the climate is unpredictable. The water in all these pools has to be kept warm. But bacteria (disease-carrying germs) breed easily in warm, wet conditions, so pool water also has to be cleaned regularly.

Keeping the heat in

Like hot tap water, the water in many pools is heated using gas or electricity, but this is very expensive. Some home pools are now heated using solar panels. Solar panels are sheets of metal that are painted black and enclosed in glass sheets. This helps them to absorb heat from the Sun's rays. The pool water is pumped through tubes in the panels to heat it up. At night, when there is no heat from the Sun's rays, the water begins to cool down. One way to prevent this happening is to cover the water surface with hollow plastic balls at night. The air inside the balls is an excellent insulator. It acts as a barrier, trapping heat in the pool water for longer.

You can have lots of fun at the world's biggest swimming pool, on the Japanese island of Kyushu.

Sparkling clean

In the autumn, outdoor pools have to be cleared of leaves. The water from any pool has to be cleaned and filtered all year round to remove dirt and rubbish. The water is pumped out of the pool through a filter unit that acts like a sieve. It is then pumped back into the pool. However, a water filter does not remove bacteria, or tiny plants called algae. These plants, if unchecked, eventually grow so much that they turn the water green. Both the bacteria and algae are killed by a chemical called chlorine – a strong bleach that is added in tiny amounts to the water.

Under the water

An aquarium is a pool for fish and underwater creatures, made out of glass or transparent plastic so that you can look inside. To take a really good look at the fish you need to get closer. To solve this problem, some modern aquariums have a walkway inside a long plastic tube, that runs along the bottom of the tank. Not only can you have a good look at the fish, but they can have a look at you, too! The circular shape of the tube makes it very strong. It is able to withstand the pressure of the water pushing on the outside.

At Osaka Aquarium in Japan, these children can get really close to all kinds of underwater creatures.

TELEVISION WORLD

When was the last time you watched television? Yesterday afternoon? Last night? This morning? We can come home at any time, switch on the television, sit back and watch any number of programmes. It is hardly surprising then that television is the most popular form of entertainment, watched by many millions of people all over the world! Colour television is the result of 50 years of research. The first televisions showed a black-and-white picture made up of only a few lines on a small circular screen. Today's colour televisions have screens of all sizes, high-quality sound and show pictures with life-like colour, enabling people to have a cinema in their own home.

Nowadays, even people who are attending an event can see the main action televised for them on enormous screens, wherever they sit or stand.

TELEVISION VIEWING

In 1926, a Scottish engineer, John Logie Baird (1886–1946), gave the first demonstration of a practical television system to members of the Royal Institute in London. Overnight he became famous, but it took another ten years before the first regular television programmes were made.

Inside a television

The back of a television screen is coated with millions of tiny dots, arranged in lines in groups of three. These dots are made of chemical substances called phosphors, which glow when struck by a beam of electrons (particles charged with negative electricity). A colour television has three beams which come from electron guns at the back of the television. When hit by the beams, one phosphor dot in each group glows red, one glows blue and the other green. When you look at the screen from a distance, your eyes merge the red, blue and green light together, to form a clear colour picture.

Television in orbit

Most television programmes are sent as signals from TV stations or transmitters, and are picked up by television aerials. These signals travel in straight lines. They cannot 'bend' over mountains or round the Earth. For this reason, different areas have their own local television stations or transmitters. However, communications satellites in space can transmit television signals all around the world. Geostationary satellites (satellites with orbits that keep them exactly over the same place on Earth) beam television programmes directly to satellite dishes. They can transmit television programmes between different countries round the world, or send many programmes to one country.

There are three electron guns at the back of a television set. They are directed onto the phosphor dots very precisely by **electromagnets**.

MIXING LIGHT

Most colours can be produced by mixing red, blue and green light in different amounts. Equal amounts of red and green light create yellow; red and blue light creates magenta; blue and green light creates cyan; all three colours together create white. All the images you see on a colour television or film are made by mixing different amounts of red, blue and green light.

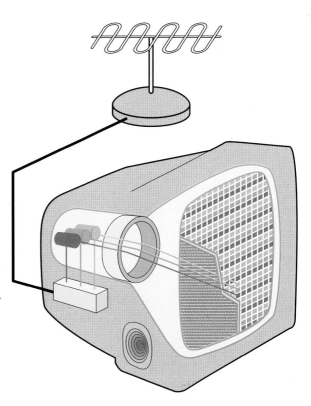

DIVE! DIVE! DIVE!

Would you like the chance to explore an underwater city or an ancient shipwreck? The ocean bed still hides all sorts of fascinating secrets. In the last 50 years, the sport of diving has gradually begun to open up this underwater world to thousands of people. The latest advances in equipment have made diving safer and more popular than it has ever been. But divers have always faced two connected problems – finding a way to breathe under water, and dealing with the crushing pressure of the water at great depths. So how do divers breathe under water?

Breathing under water

The deeper a diver goes under the ocean, the greater the weight, or pressure, of the water on his or her chest, and the harder it is to breathe. This problem has been solved for people diving down to about 30 metres by the invention of SCUBA (Self Contained Underwater Breathing Apparatus). The diver breathes air that has been forced, or compressed, into a steel tank, at about 300 times **atmospheric pressure**. Before this air passes into the diver's mouthpiece, it goes though a **valve**, which reduces the pressure until it exactly matches the pressure of the surrounding waters. This enables the diver to breathe easily.

SCUBA

A French naval officer, Jacques Ives Cousteau (b.1910), perfected the aqualung diving apparatus (1943), now called SCUBA. It enabled him, and countless others that followed him, to explore under water, free from the heavy traditional diving suit.

SCUBA divers have explored coral reefs, underwater caves, glaciers, as well as just enjoying seeing underwater life close up.

Decompression

One of the gases in the air we breathe is called nitrogen. When divers are deep under water, high pressure causes the nitrogen in their air supply to dissolve in their blood. When they return to the surface the nitrogen is released. If they come back up suddenly, the nitrogen is released too quickly and the divers suffer a paralysing condition called the bends. Returning to the surface slowly lets nitrogen leave the body harmlessly. This process is called decompression.

BARREL SUIT

In 1721, John Lethbridge invented a diving suit shaped like a barrel. It had two holes for arms and a glass peephole, so the diver could see under water. The diver lay face-down, and had to return to the surface to breathe.

UNDER PRESSURE

Although we cannot feel it, the weight of the air above us presses down on our bodies. This pressure is measured in atmospheres. On dry land, the air we breathe normally has a pressure of 1 atmosphere. Water pressure is also measured in atmospheres. The further down you go under the water, the greater the pressure. In the ocean, water pressure increases by 1 atmosphere every 10 metres.

In 1960, the *Bathyscaphe* descended 11km (8 miles) into the Marianas Trench, the deepest part of the Pacific Ocean, where the water pressure is more than 1000 atmospheres. The spherical shape of the *Bathyscaphe* made it strong enough to withstand water pressure which would crush any ordinary vessel.

SAIL POWER

When you think of sailing, do you picture a small dinghy or yacht cutting across the waves, sails stretched in the breeze? Sailing can be a very relaxing pastime, but it is not always like this. Ice yachts which 'sail' on ice are the fastest of all sail-powered crafts, sometimes achieving speeds of over 225 kph (140 mph). The fastest sailing vessels on water regularly reach about 80 kph (50 mph), often in winds of no more than about 32 kph (20 mph). So how is this possible?

Modern sailing vessels, like this catamaran and sailboard, are built from tough, light materials. Their design cleverly uses the driving force of the wind, and the resistance of the water in which they float to get the maximum possible forward speed.

TRIANGLE OF FORCES

A sailing yacht 'reaches' or sails across the wind. The wind pushing on the sails produces a force that acts in two directions. It pushes the yacht forwards and also tries to push it sideways at the same time. The yacht's centre board, or keel, resists the sideways push and converts it into a forward pushing force. The three forces – the wind, the sideways force, and resulting forward force – acting together are called the **triangle of forces**.

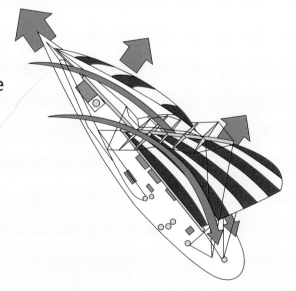

Tough materials

Modern sailing vessels are built from tough, lightweight materials for greater strength and speed. The hulls of sailing dinghies such as the International Laser are built out of GRP (glass-reinforced plastic). GRP consists of layers of matting made from fine strands of glass. The layers of matting are cut to shape and placed in a mould, then soaked in a synthetic resin – a liquid, plastic material which sets very hard. Together, the resin and glass fibres make a very strong material. The different parts of the hull are made in separate moulds and are then glued together. This makes the hull watertight. As long as the hull remains undamaged, these boats are almost unsinkable.

More than 100,000 International Lasers have been built. These fast racing dinghies are constructed from glass-fibre, and are virtually unsinkable. Their **spars** are made of **aluminium** alloys or carbon fibre, and their sails from Mylar – a strong synthetic plastic material.

LAND YACHTS

In Mauritania, sail powered craft running on railway tracks race along at high speeds. These specialized land yachts achieve speeds over 161 kph (100 mph), but they are easily blown over because they run on rails. They cannot be steered out of danger of capsizing like a sailboat can.

WAVE ACTION

What does the phrase, 'a day at the beach' mean to you? For some people, a day at the beach means a day in the sun, fishing, swimming, playing beach games and relaxing. For others it means a day pitting their skills against the waves. If the waves are big enough, surfers balancing on surfboards can ride them at astonishing speed, keeping just ahead of the crest of the wave. Further out to sea, sailboarders can test their strength against the energy of the wind and waves. What causes the waves, and why can surfers go so fast?

Wind and waves

If you look at the waves coming in towards the beach, you will notice that in deeper water the waves travel towards the shore, usually without breaking. But as they ride up towards the shore, they tumble over and crash onto the beach. This is because the bottom of the wave is dragged along the sand and slowed down, but the top of the wave continues at speed, so it topples over in the shallower water on the beach.

TSUNAMIS

Violent storms or underwater earthquakes can cause freak waves more than 30 metres high. These waves are popularly called tidal waves, but scientists prefer the Japanese name, *tsunamis*, because such waves are not caused by tides. Tsunamis are created far out at sea, and can become very dangerous. As they approach land they speed up and may cause great destruction on the shore.

These surfers in Hawaii, USA, manage to keep just ahead of the waves, that push them at incredible speeds.

Small and fast

Surfboards and sailboards plane. This means they skim over the surface of the water. They can go as fast as the person riding them dares! In fact, some boards are so small and light they will not float when the rider is stationary because they are not **buoyant** enough – they sink under the rider's weight. They can only support their rider when travelling on the crest of a wave at great speed, because they can plane or skim on top of the surface.

Modern sand yachts that can top 124 kph (78 mph) first appeared in Belgium in the 1920s. However, in the 4th century BC, the Emperor Liang Yuan Ti of China had a wind cart made that could carry 30 passengers.

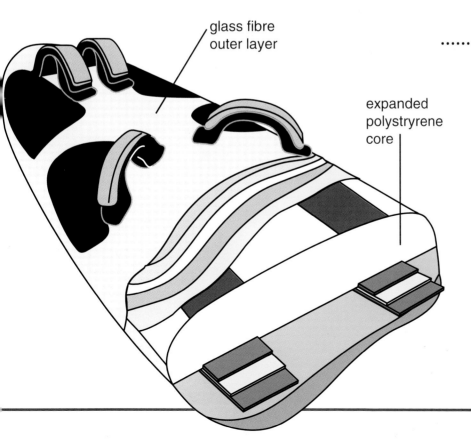

glass fibre outer layer

expanded polystryrene core

A surfboard must be strong and lightweight. The inside, or core, is made of expanded polystyrene, a foam-like plastic that can be carved accurately into any shape. Glass fibre and carbon fibre on the outside make boards strong enough to withstand the beating of the waves.

FREE AS A BIRD

Have you ever dreamed that you could fly? Flying a hang-glider must be the nearest thing to it! Experienced hang-glider pilots have been launched from hot-air balloons, towed into the air like ordinary gliders, or have jumped over cliffs. When they are airborne, hang-glider pilots seek out rising currents of warmer air called thermals. Once caught in a thermal, the hang-glider may rise many thousands of metres into the air, and is capable of flying great distances.

Strength and balance

Hang-gliders have an **aluminium** frame shaped like the letter A, that is both strong and light. Depending on the type of glider, the wing is formed by stretching flexible or rigid material over the A-frame. The pilot is suspended from a harness below the wing, safely attached to it by a karabiner – a strong metal clip. This special clip was originally invented for mountaineers who use it to attach themselves to ropes. Because it is closed by a spring, it can be quickly released.

THERMALS

Thermals often happen in warm, thundery weather. Air is heated by the sun and rises because it is lighter than the surrounding cold air. The cold air pushes under the warm air causing it to rise. Thermals help gliders fly long distances by lifting them up high in the sky. Gliders cannot climb by themselves and drop quickly if they are not being lifted by a thermal.

The pilot steers the glider by holding onto a triangular frame and making side-to-side body movements.

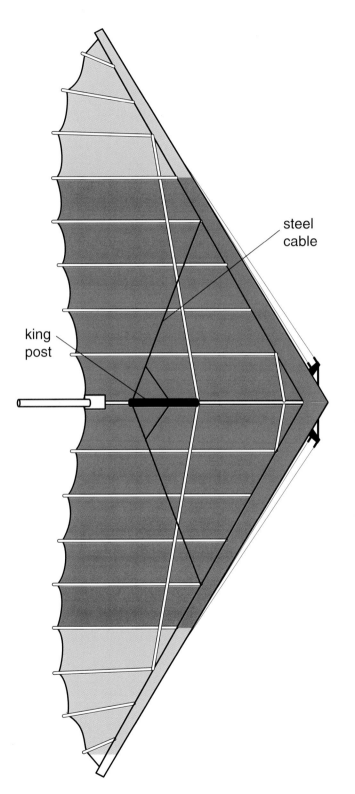

king
post

steel
cable

A hang-glider is made even stronger by steel cables stretched under tension (very tightly) to the wing and a post at the centre called the king post. The cables prevent the wing from bending too much and breaking. Weights are placed on the wing to test it for strength. These weights are equal to six times any force that the hang-glider is likely to encounter.

EARLY GLIDERS

Otto Lilienthal (1849–96), a German, made hundreds of short flights in homemade gliders that he designed and built out of willow and cotton. He launched himself from hill tops, and controlled his direction by body movements, like modern hang-glider pilots. Lilienthal had studied bird-flight closely and his machines were very similar to the first designs for a flying machine, sketched by the great artist and sculptor Leonardo da Vinci in about 1487. Before his death in a flying accident in 1896, Lilienthal made a flight of more than 350 metres.

GLOSSARY

acoustics the science of sound

alloy a mixture of two or more metals

aluminium a very light, strong metal

atmospheric pressure the weight of the air around us

binary digits a system of numbers using only 0 and 1 to represent all the numbers instead of units, tens and hundreds, etc. For example, 1 is 001, 2 is 0010, 4 is 0100.

buoyant capable of floating

cable strong wires by which force is used to control or operate a mechanism

camping gas a mixture of gases in a small strong container, used for cooking or light

cantilevers supporting link between brake cables and brake pads

carbon fibre a very pure and fine fibre made of carbon. It is used to reinforce plastic materials to make them strong.

centripetal force the force you feel when you whirl a weight on string round and round

chromium a metal mixed with steel to make it stainless

electromagnet core of magnetic material surrounded by a coil of wire, through which an electric current is passed to magnetize the core

fibreglass strong plastic material reinforced with matting made from finely spun glass fibres, sometimes called GRP or glass reinforced plastic

friction the rubbing of one thing against another and the force that resists this

graphics picture produced by a computer

gravity a force or pull between any two objects such as the Earth and an apple falling towards it

hydraulic a mechanism, such as a brake, operated by a liquid in a pipe

insulator a material that keeps you warm because it does not conduct heat

kilojoules joules are units used by scientists to measure work or energy; a kilojoule is a 1000 of them

molybdenum a metal added to steel to make it tougher

nylon a touch, lightweight plastic material used to make fabrics

Olympic Games a sports meeting, first held in Ancient Greece. It now takes place every 4 years and athletes from all over the world compete

paragliding sport using a special, steerable parachute

perspiration sweat

satellite a kind of automatic television station sent into space by rocket to travel round the world to transmit television pictures back to Earth, also used for telephone transmission

spar in this case, the mast used to support the sail

synthetic produced artificially rather than occurring naturally

titanium a metal added to steel to make it strong and able to withstand high temperatures

transistor an electronic device that is used to amplify an electric current or switch it on and off

triangle of forces a method used by physicists to add to the effect of two forces acting in different directions

valve a device like a tap used to turn something, such as air or water, on and off and control its flow

virtual reality pictures controlled or generated by a computer which appear to be real and in which the viewer seems to be involved

water vapour water in a misty or gas-like state like the water in your breath on a cold morning

FACT FILE

- The first computer game to go on sale was developed in 1971 by Nolan Bushnell, a young American engineer. It was called *Computer Space*, and barely sold 2000 copies. Bushnell's next game, *Pong*, a form of table tennis, was a huge success and sold more than 100,000 copies. Bushnell went on to found Atari, the computer firm.

- Hang-gliding started when an American, Francis Melvin Rogallo, designed a strong, flexible wing in 1948. But it was an Australian engineer, Bill Moyes, who produced the familiar delta-shaped wing. In 1969, Moyes' partner, Bill Bennet, tested the design. He was towed on water skis and took off to fly over the Statue of Liberty.

- Captain Cooke, the explorer and navigator, described surfing in Hawaii in 1771. Surfing became popular in California during the 1950s and 1960s.

- The longest sailing vessel ever built is the French *Club Med 1*. This ship has five aluminium masts, and the 232 square metres (2500 square feet) of sails are computer-controlled. However, the *Cheng Ho*, a massive Chinese vessel built in about 1420, is believed to have had nine masts.

- The earliest bicycle race (for which records exist) took place at the Parc de St Cloud, Paris, France in 1868.

- Sega, Sony and five other large entertainment companies are involved in location-based entertainment centres, or LBEs. These provide cinemas, theme park rides and video arcades in one place. Cinetropolis centres are an example of an LBE. Here, film rides are shown on wrap around screens. The seats are co-ordinated to move with the film, about a metre in any direction – enough to give anyone the illusion of terrifying movement!

INDEX